Level 2
REPERTOIRE
Exploring Piano Classics
A Masterwork Method for the Developing Pianist

NANCY BACHUS

ISBN-10: 0-7390-5559-3
ISBN-13: 978-0-7390-5559-5

Alfred

TO THE TEACHER

About the *Exploring Piano Classics* Series

Exploring Piano Classics: A Masterworks Method for Developing Pianists pairs motivating performance repertoire with thoughtful technical studies. Each level contains two books:

■ *Exploring Piano Classics—Repertoire* includes pieces from the major style periods. The repertoire was selected and graded by studying festival, competition, and examination lists from the United States, Canada, and the United Kingdom. Background information on each style period, its instruments, composers, and the music itself is included. The CD performances of the repertoire in each level provide an indispensable auditory learning tool for appropriate musical interpretation.

■ *Exploring Piano Classics—Technique* includes **basic keyboard patterns**— five-finger patterns, scales, chords, cadences, and arpeggios in the major and minor keys found in the *Repertoire* book. These patterns can be developed into a daily warm-up routine for each practice session while expanding the student's technical skills. **Exercises and etudes**, an important feature of the *Technique* book, were chosen and written to develop basic keyboard touches and other necessary technical skills for mastering each piece. Suggestions for efficient practice are also included.

These companion books include a convenient page-by-page correlation, allowing the teacher to assign pages in the *Technique* book that reinforce the music that students are learning in the *Repertoire* book. When used together, the books give students a deep understanding of the art of music, performance practices, and the necessary skills to play the piano with technical ease. The knowledge, skills and joy experienced in the study of music through this series will enrich students throughout their lives.

CONTENTS

During the Renaissance, Baroque, and Classical Eras

The Renaissance (ca. 1400–1600) and Baroque Eras (1600–1750)

The *Renaissance* era marks the beginning of modern times. *Baroque* describes a style of art and music in a period when artists and musicians worked for **patrons** like **King Louis XIV** (1638-1715) who asked them to create specific works.

The earliest **harpsichords** (keyboard instruments with strings plucked by quills) appeared around 1400 during the Renaissance era. The **virginal** (also called **virginals**) was popular in European homes from 1500-1700, from the Renaissance into the Baroque Era.

16th-century engraving of a woman playing a virginal

Virginal or Virginals

A **virginal** was a small harpsichord with one keyboard. The bass strings (longest) were at the front, so it could be built in different shapes—rectangular or polygonal.

- In England, the term virginals was used for all harpsichords.

- English composers from around 1550 to 1650 created the first harpsichord music, which was the forerunner to piano music.

- The style was different from organ or vocal music. It was technically difficult with fast scales, broken chords, and octaves.

Viennese style piano (1795) One lever controls dampers; one is a mute stop

The Classical Era (1750–1820)

The term *Classical* is used to describe a late 18th-century style of European music. Dances from royal courts influenced the keyboard music.

Early Piano Pedals

The new pianoforte, invented around 1700, was widely used by the 1770s.

- The earliest pianos had **hand stops** that could raise and lower the dampers.

- By the 1760s, these were replaced by **knee levers**.

During the Romantic and Modern Eras

*1803 Érard (four-pedal) piano
owned by Beethoven*

The Romantic (1790–1910) and Modern (1880–forward) Eras

The term *Romantic* is used to describe 19th-century art, literary writing, and music. Romantic artists expressed their personal ideas and emotions in dramatic music and artwork.

Around 1900, there were **many different styles of music and art**. Many artists painted ordinary people in their daily lives. Musicians became interested in folk music of their own and foreign cultures.

Early 19th-Century Piano Pedals

By 1800, **foot pedals** had replaced hand levers.

- The damper pedal was only used occasionally as a "special effect" until the Romantic era when composers began writing for its almost constant use to create new sounds and colors.

- An *una corda* (soft) pedal shifted the keyboard and hammers to the right so it would strike fewer strings.

- Some pianos also had a **moderator pedal** to "modify" or change the tone quality by placing fabric between the strings and hammers.

- The **bassoon pedal** was also common at that time. It placed a roll of paper and silk cloth over the bass strings, creating a buzzing sound.

Sostenuto Pedal

In 1874, the American Steinway company patented a **sostenuto** (tone-sustaining) pedal and installed it on their instruments.

- Soon other manufacturers were doing the same.

- Today **three pedals**—damper on the right, *una corda* on the left, and sostenuto in the middle—are standard on grand pianos.

- True working sostenuto pedals are found less often on upright pianos.

20th-century piano with three pedals

6

Use with *Exploring Piano Classics—Technique*, Level 2
Warm-Up Patterns in C Major, pp. 6–9, Increasing Speed with Slur Groups, p. 10

The Tarantella

Frederick Scotson Clark spent most of his life in London, England. His **tarantella** has the character of the original energetic folk dance. One couple danced, accompanying themselves with castanets and tambourines, while onlookers sometimes sang.

Tarantella in C Major

Frederick Scotson Clark
(1840–1883)

Romantic Melody

Félix Le Couppey was a French pianist and teacher. This beautiful *Melody in C,* typical of Romantic-style music, should be played with rich, legato tone.

Melody in C
No. 21 from *A. B. C. for the Piano*

Félix Le Couppey
(1811–1887)

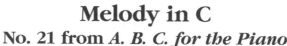

ROMANTIC

8

RENAISSANCE

Elizabethan England

Elizabeth I (1533-1603) became Queen of England in 1558 during the late Renaissance. Her reign has been called the **Elizabethan era**, a time of great political and cultural achievements.

■ During her reign, the Englishman **Sir Frances Drake** (ca. 1545-1596) was the first to sail completely around the world (1577-1580).

■ Music was so important at this time that Sir Drake took a string quartet of musicians with him on his ship, *The Golden Hind*.

■ Queen Elizabeth not only supported the arts, but was known to be an excellent dancer and musician herself.

■ She attended many performances of **William Shakespeare's** (1564–1616) plays.

■ She not only sang, but also performed on the **lute** (similar to a guitar, only with a pear-shaped body), and the **virginals.**

Queen Elizabeth I playing the Lute

In England, the term **air (ayre)** means "song" or "tune." It was also used to describe a song for one singer, many with accompaniment arranged for a lute. *Old English Air* moves from major to minor, typical of Renaissance keyboard music.

Queen Elizabeth's Virginal

Old English Air

Track 3

3

Anonymous
(16th century)

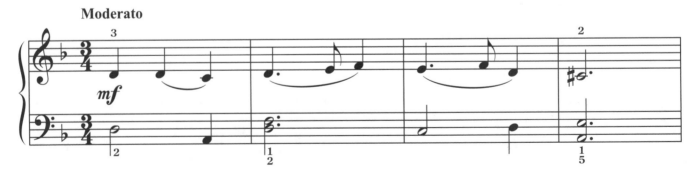

Warm-Up Patterns in D Major, pp. 12–15, Larger Intervals, p. 17, Two-Note Slurs and Staccato, p. 17

The Country Dance

Johann Christian Bach, a son of Johann Sebastian Bach (1685-1750), became known as the "London Bach" since most of his professional life was spent there.

- An English **rustic line dance** or **country dance**, which was popular in the French court of Louis XIV, was given the French name **contredanse**. Its popularity then spread to other European courts.

- Opening with a curtsy or bow, couples danced complicated steps and exchanged positions without missing a beat.

Country Dance (1745)
by William Hogarth (1697–1764)

CLASSICAL

Rustic Dance

Track 4

Johann Christian Bach
(1735-1782)

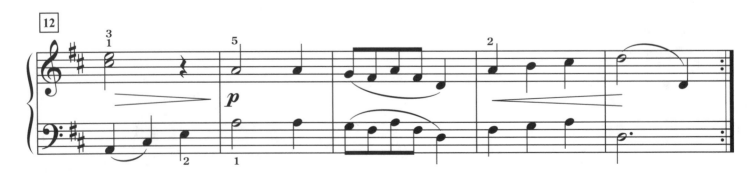

Carlos de Seixas

Carlos de Seixas, the leading Portuguese composer of the 18th century, was the organist at the Royal Chapel in Lisbon from age 16 until his death. He composed more than 700 keyboard pieces.

■ **Minuets** were graceful, gliding dances popular for 150 years.

■ Play all quarter notes not marked with a slur slightly detached.

BAROQUE

Track 5

Minuet in C Minor

Carlos de Seixas
(1704-1742)

Warm-Up Patterns in F Major, pp. 18–21, More about Two-Note Slurs, p. 22

The Arioso

Many keyboard students in the late-18th century learned from **Johann Gottlob Türk's** *School of Keyboard Playing.* This **arioso** (a short song or instrumental piece) is from a set of pieces Türk wrote to go along with his course.

Arioso

Track 6

Johann Gottlob Türk
(1750–1813)

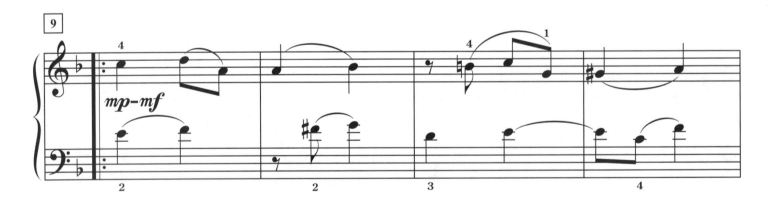

Vladimir Rebikov

Vladimir Rebikov was one of the first Russian composers to experiment with unusual harmonies and scales. He uses them here to create a picture in sound from an Asian culture.

Track 7

The Chinese Doll

Vladimir Rebikov
(1866–1920)

MODERN

14

Warm-Up Patterns in D Minor, pp. 12–15, The Damper Pedal, p. 23, Creating Different Moods, p. 24

Cornelius Gurlitt

Cornelius Gurlitt was a German composer best known today for his short pieces for young piano students.

- He studied organ, piano and composition in Germany, Denmark, and Italy, and also performed in these places.

- He believed the purpose of music was to educate, not entertain.

- Although the title *Night Journey* was not given by Gurlitt, by using imagination, the performer can tell a story in sound, typical of Romantic music.

The Great Railway *(1844)*
by Joseph Mallord William Turner (1775–1851)

Night Journey
from *First Steps of the Young Pianist*

Track 8

Cornelius Gurlitt (1820-1901)
Op. 82, No. 65

ROMANTIC

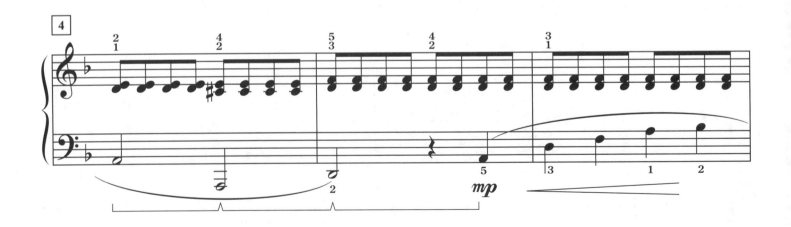

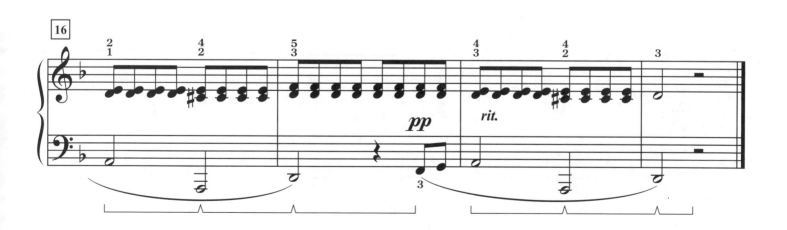

Jean Louis Streabbog

The Belgian composer and pianist **Jean Louis Streabbog** wrote more than 1,000 piano pieces. Many of them are **etudes** (studies) for a particular technique such as broken chords or hand crossing. His real name was Jean Louis **Gobbaerts** (spelled backward, it is Streabbog, his pen name).

Distant Bells

Track 9

Jean Louis Streabbog (1835–1886)
Op. 63, No. 6

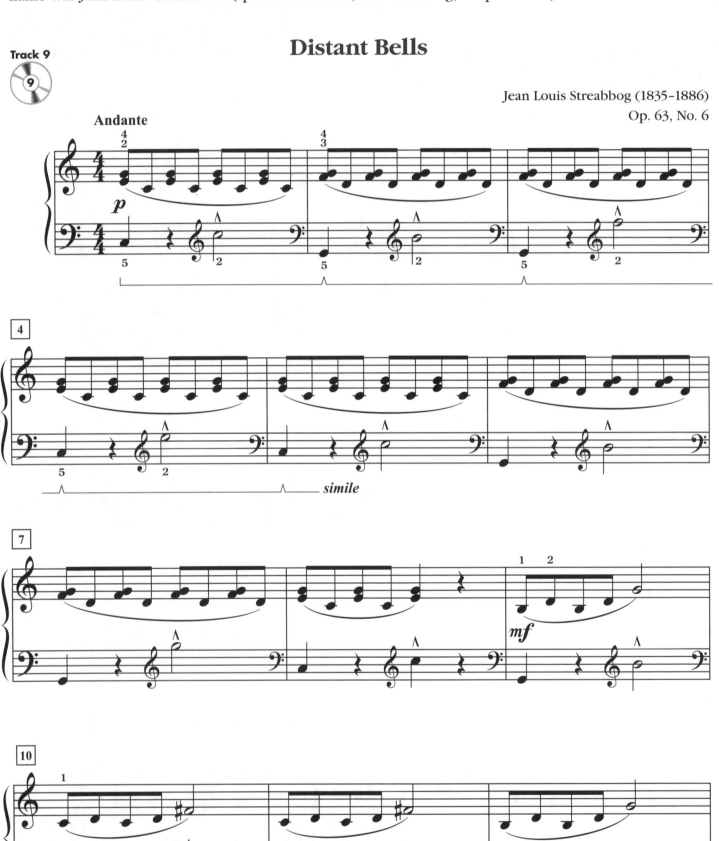

18

Dances in the 18th Century

Dancing was a necessary skill for 18th-century ladies and gentlemen and was popular in all levels of society.

- **Franz Joseph Haydn** (1732–1809) composed dances throughout his career with many published in his lifetime.

- The **quadrille** was a type of *contredanse*. Four couples, arranged in a square, danced difficult steps.

- The music was usually in repeated sections of 8–16 measures.

- Play the grace notes in measures 17, 21 and 29 ahead of the beat.

Franz Joseph Haydn

Quadrille

Track 10

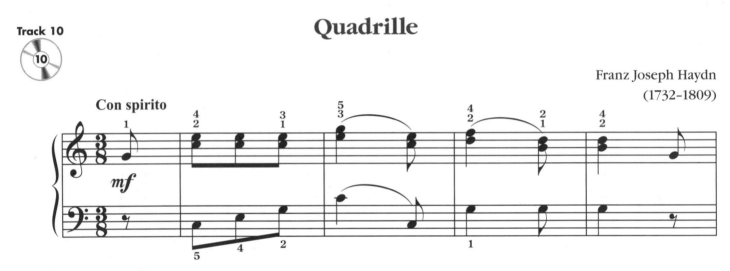

Franz Joseph Haydn
(1732–1809)

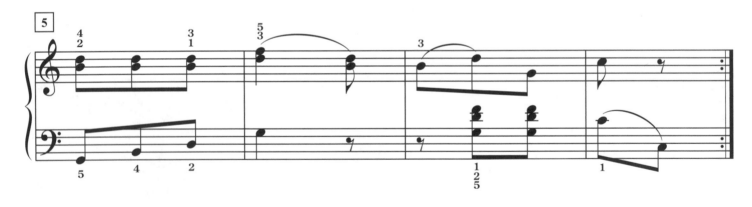

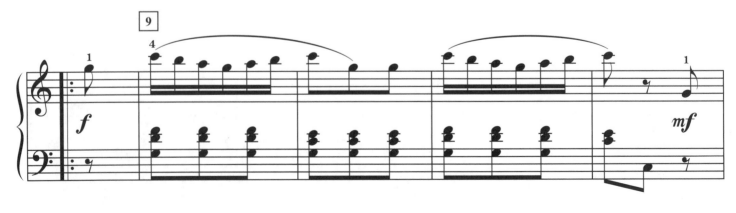

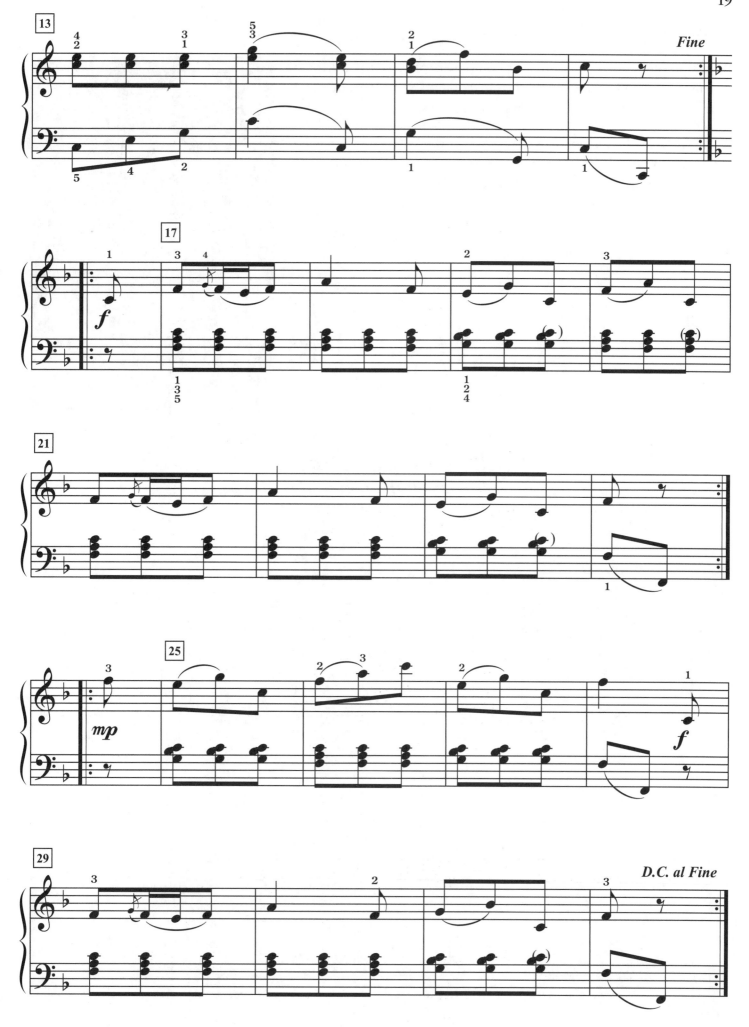

Béla Bartók

Béla Bartók is one of the greatest composers of the early 20th century. He combined Romantic style elements with ingredients of Hungarian folk music, creating powerful new music.

- ■ When Bartók was only seven, his father died. His mother was a piano teacher who kept moving to find work for herself and the best musical training for her son.

- ■ Living in different places as a child, Bartók heard many types of what he called "peasant music"—music of people who worked on farms in rural areas.

Béla Bartók, age 5, when he began piano lessons

Swineherd's Dance
No. 12 from *First Term at the Piano*

Track 11

11

Béla Bartók
(1881–1945)

Allegro

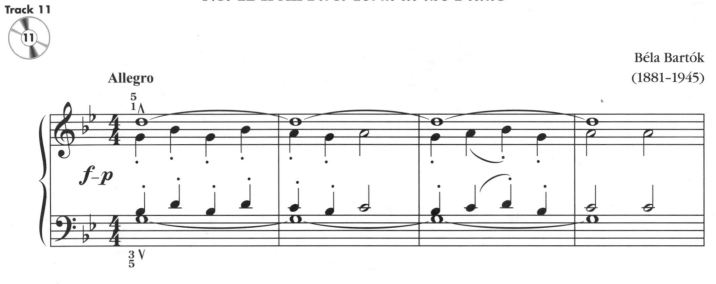

5

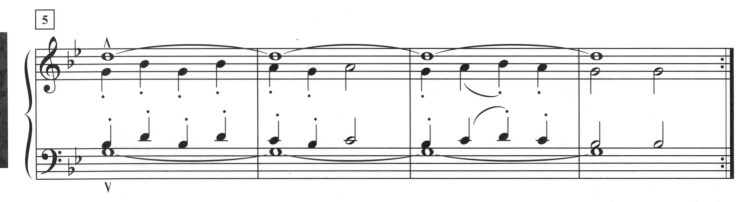

MODERN

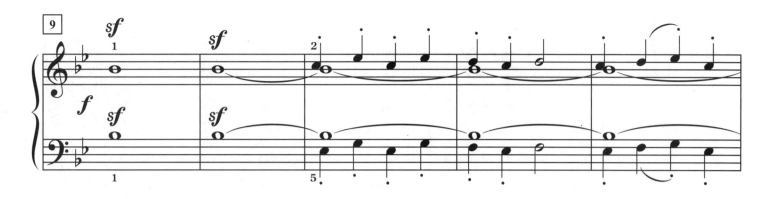

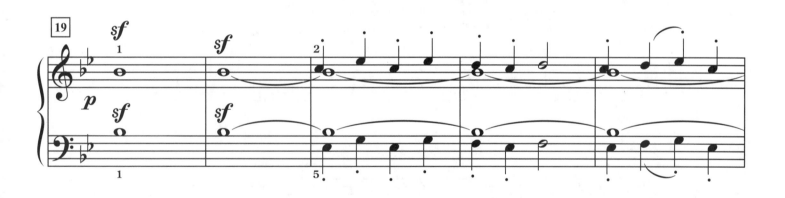

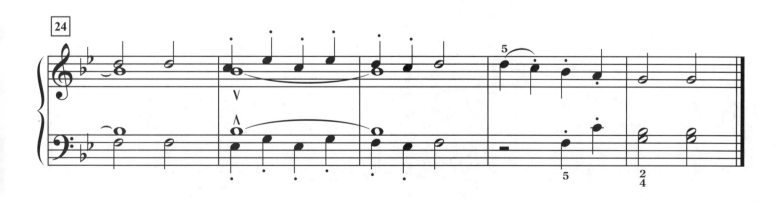

The Minuet

Social status was closely related to dancing the minuet in the 18th century. Not only were clothing and jewels on display, but a person's reputation could rise or fall by their grace and skill.

- The moderately slow minuet was usually danced by one couple while everyone else watched. "Honors" or a series of bows and curtseys to the partner and audience opened the dance.

- The basic minuet pattern took six beats, so a natural accent falls every two measures.

- Play all LH quarter notes not marked with a slur slightly detached.

Minuet in C Major

Track 12

George Adam Kress
(1744–1788)

Arcangelo Corelli

Born in Italy, **Arcangelo Corelli** was a violinist whose string works were published, sold, and performed in many countries during his lifetime. He wrote only a few keyboard pieces.

The **sarabande** was a serious and dignified Baroque dance where the dancer frequently used hand castanets.

Arcangelo Corelli

BAROQUE

Track 13

Sarabande

Arcangelo Corelli
(1653–1713)

JOHANN SEBASTIAN BACH

BAROQUE

The Bach family of musicians was active in German musical life for about 300 years (1550–1845) with **Johann Sebastian Bach** being the greatest of them all.

- Orphaned at 10, Bach left his home in Eisenach to live with his older brother.

- At 15, carrying all he owned, Bach made a difficult 200-mile journey to Lünberg where "poor boys with good treble voices" could receive a free education and room and board for singing in the church choir.

- At 18, he was hired to play for church services in Arnstadt.

- An early work, his *Suite in G Minor,* BWV 822, was written somewhere between 1700 and 1703.

J. S. Bach around the age of 30

Minuet in G Minor
from *Suite in G Minor*

Track 14

Johann Sebastian Bach (1685–1750)

BWV 822

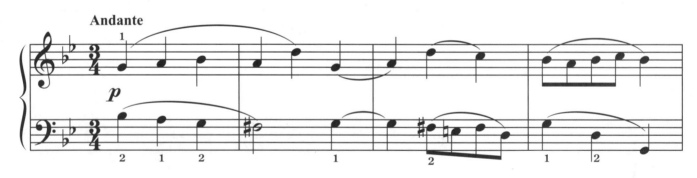

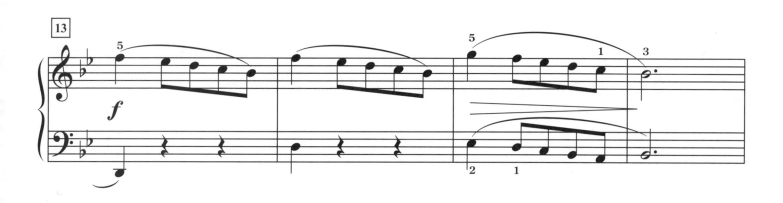

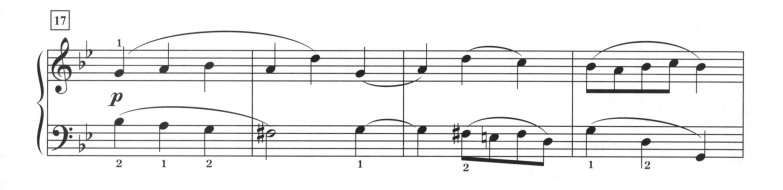

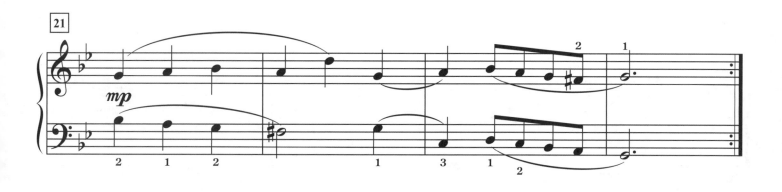

26

Igor Stravinsky

Igor Stravinsky (1882–1971), a major composer of the 20th century, wrote the music for some of the most exciting ballets of all time.

He composed several piano pieces built on five-finger patterns for beginning pianists. In *Lento,* the right hand plays patterns in D major and F major with a simple left-hand accompaniment.

*Drawing of Stravinsky
by Pablo Picasso (1881–1973)*

Track 15

Lento
No. 6 from *Les cinq doigts* **(The Five Fingers)**

Igor Stravinsky
(1882–1971)

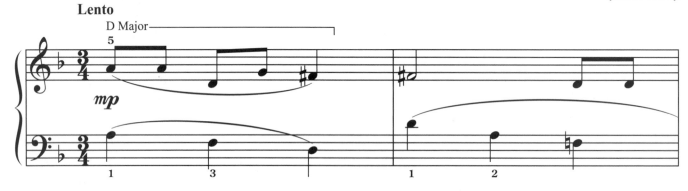

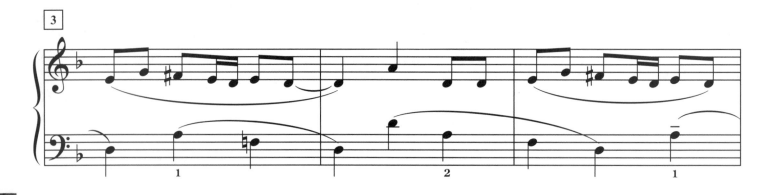

MODERN

LUDWIG VAN BEETHOVEN

"He [Beethoven] is greatly admired for the speed of his playing, and … masters the greatest difficulties."
—Newspaper in Vienna, around 1790

Portrait of a young Beethoven

Ludwig van Beethoven was one of the first composers to earn a living as a performer and by publishing his own works. He received money from aristocrats, but not one specific patron.

- Wanting to create a child prodigy like Mozart, Beethoven's father forced him to practice many hours a day when he was only four. A neighbor said the young Beethoven often cried.

- Studying harpsichord, organ, violin, horn, and composition, he played his first concert at age 8, had his first composition published at 11, and was hired as a court keyboard player at 12.

- When Beethoven was about 20, Franz Joseph Haydn visited Bonn, Germany (Beethoven's birthplace and where he spent his early years). Soon after, Beethoven traveled to Vienna to study with this famous man and made it his home.

Asked by a publisher to arrange popular European folk songs, this *Russian Folk Song,* Op. 107, No. 7, is the **theme** for a set of variations written for piano solo, or as an accompaniment for flute or violin.

- The text of *Beautiful Minka* is about a Russian soldier leaving for war.

- It tells of his girlfriend's sorrow, their vows to remain faithful, and his promise to return as a hero.

Beethoven's monument in Bonn, Germany

Russian Folk Song
("Beautiful Minka")

Ludwig van Beethoven (1770–1827)
Op. 107, No. 7

CLASSICAL

Warm-Up Patterns in D Minor, pp. 12–15, Chords and Rapid Melodies, p. 40

The Tarantella Legend

Twentieth-century composers, like the Russian **Alexander Goedicke**, use many forms, including the 500-year-old **tarantella**. The legend that this dance was a cure for the bite of a poisonous tarantula spider is no longer accepted.

Tarantella in D Minor

Track 17

Alexander Goedicke
(1877–1957)

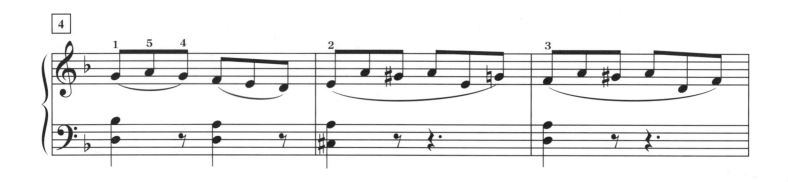

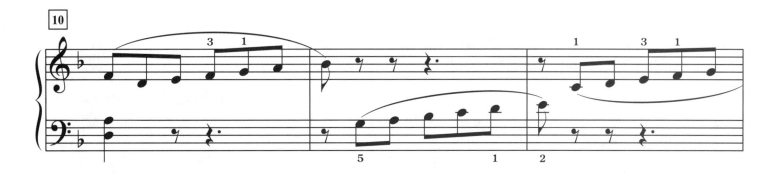

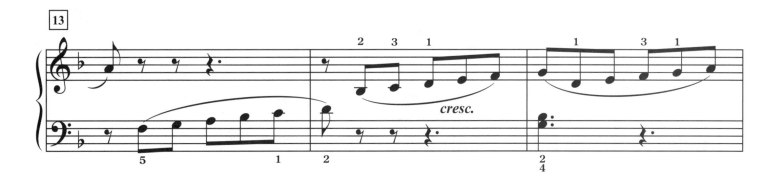

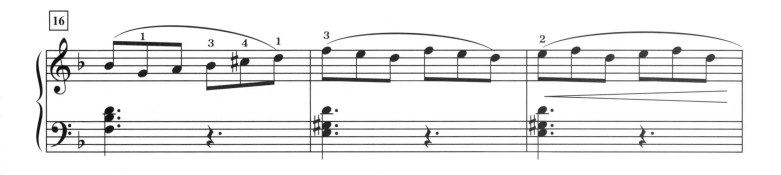

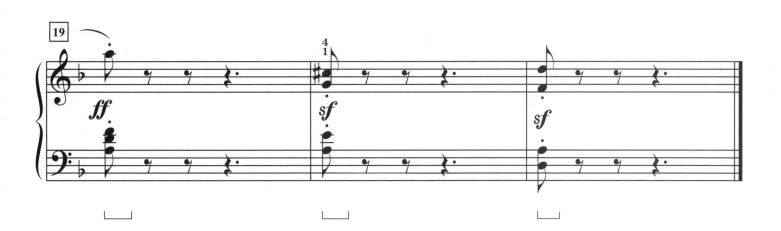

Carl Reinecke

Carl Reinecke (1824-1910) was a respected composer and teacher whose **elegy** (originally a reflective poem, frequently mourning a death) creates a feeling of sorrow and sadness.

- Born in Denmark, he was taught by his father, a music teacher who also taught **Cornelius Gurlitt** (1820-1901).

- Carl then became an influential teacher himself in Germany, teaching **Edvard Grieg** (1843-1907) and **Isaac Albéniz** (1860-1909).

Carl Reinecke

Track 18

Elegy

Carl Reinecke (1824-1910)
Op. 183, No. 2

Andante con moto

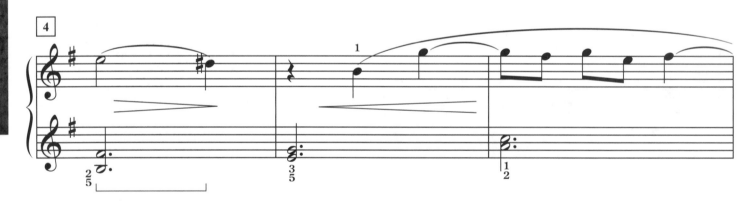

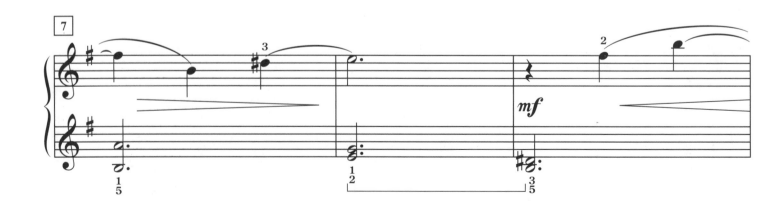

Warm-Up Patterns in A Minor, pp. 35–38, More Repeated Chords, p. 46

Exoticism

Theodor Oesten was a German composer and teacher whose piano pieces were very popular during his lifetime. Like many Romantic composers, he created the atmosphere of a foreign culture—that of Spain—in this piece. This in known as **exoticism.**

Track 19

Spanish Dance

Theodor Oesten (1813–1870)

Op. 61, No. 10

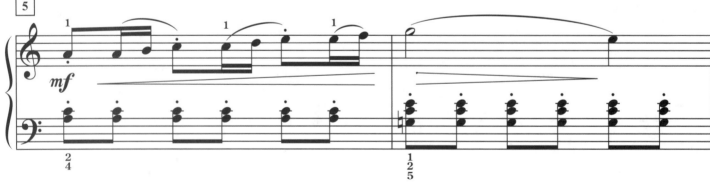

ROMANTIC

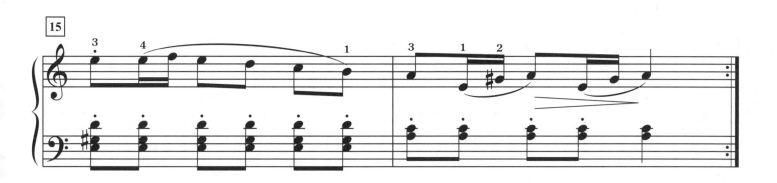

36

Warm-Up Patterns in D Major, pp. 12–15, Combining Touches, p. 47

BAROQUE

Jeremiah Clarke and King William III

Jeremiah Clarke (ca. 1673-1707) was a choirboy at the Chapel Royal in London. Around 1700, he became the director of the choirs and organist for St. Paul's Cathedral. He composed several collections of harpsichord pieces as well as sacred music.

In 1689, **William III** (1650-1702) became King of England and reigned with his wife, **Queen Mary II** (1662-1694) until her death.

- In 1693, a **Royal Charter** was issued to establish a college in their American colonies in Williamsburg, Virginia.

- The **College of William and Mary** educated 16 individuals who signed the Declaration of Independence, and is a highly respected university today.

- Play all LH quarter notes not marked with a slur slightly detached.

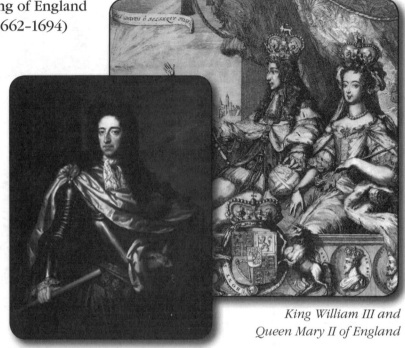

King William III

King William III and Queen Mary II of England

King William's March

Track 20

Jeremiah Clarke
(ca. 1673-1707)

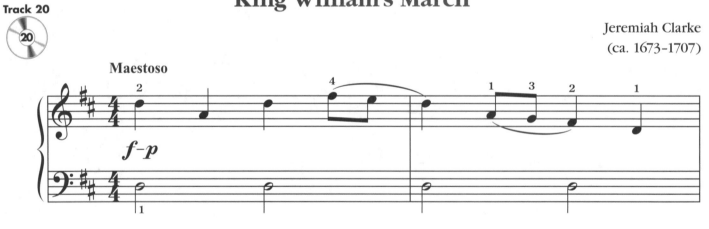

Alternating Hands, p. 48

Alexander Tcherepnin

Born in Russia, Alexander Tcherepnin lived and taught in Paris, Japan, China, and the United States. He conducted and performed as a pianist throughout Europe and in the Soviet Union.

■ Tcherepnin's mother was his first music teacher. He could read music before he knew the alphabet.

■ By age 15, he had composed an opera, a ballet, and many piano pieces, including his popular *Bagatelles*, Op. 5.

Alexander Tcherepnin

Chimes

Track 21

Alexander Tcherepnin
(1899–1977)

Vigorously and well marked

CHIMES (from *Contemporary Piano Literature, Book 2*) by ALEXANDER TCHEREPNIN

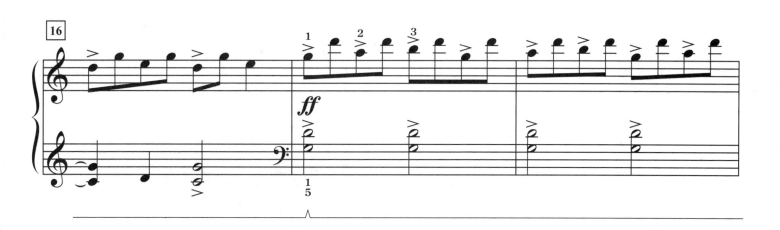

Program Music

Oskar Bolck creates a sound image of a
late-Renaissance peasants' dance
like the one depicted at right.

Warm-Up Patterns in A Major, pp. 35–38, Melody and Ostinato Bass, p. 48

The Peasant Dance *(ca. 1568)*
by *Pieter Bruegel (1525–1569)*

Track 22

Peasant Dance

Oskar Bolck
(1837–1888)

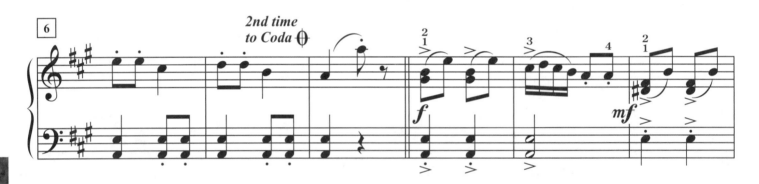

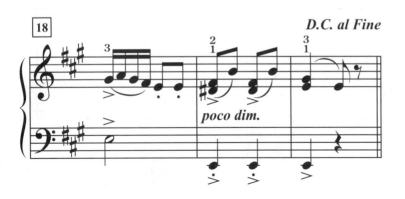

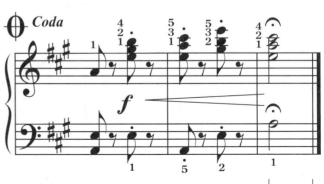

ROMANTIC